11/06

STARS in the SPOTLIGHT

Usher

Colleen Adams

PowerKiDS
press.

New York

Published in 2007 by The Rosen Publishing Group, Inc.
29 East 21st Street, New York, NY 10010

Book Design: Haley Wilson

Photo Credits: Cover, p. 20 © Frank Micelotta/Getty Images; p. 4 © Frazer Harrison/Getty Images; pp. 6, 18 © Peter Kramer/Getty Images; p. 8 © Matthew Peyton/Getty Images; pp. 10, 12, 28 © Vince Bucci/Getty Images; p. 14 © Joe Raedle/Getty Images; p. 16 © Scott Gries/Image Direct; p. 22 © Scott Gries/Getty Images; p. 24 © Elsa/Getty Images; p. 26 © Kevin Winters/Getty Images.

Library of Congress Cataloging-in-Publication Data

Adams, Colleen.
  Usher / Colleen Adams.
      p. cm. — (Stars in the spotlight)
  Includes index.
  ISBN-13: 978-1-4042-3516-7
  ISBN-10: 1-4042-3516-7 (library binding)
  1. Usher—Juvenile literature. 2. Singers—United States—Biography-—Juvenile literature. I. Title.
II. Series.
  ML3930.U84A33 2007
  782.421643092--dc22
  [B]
                              2006017748

Manufactured in the United States of America

Contents

4

A Man of Many Talents

Usher is an American singer, songwriter, dancer, and record **producer**. He has also acted on television programs and in movies. Usher had a recording contract by the time he was 14. He soon earned the respect of fans and music **critics** with his singing talent. Today he is known as one of the leading rhythm and blues (R&B) recording artists. Usher has won five Grammy Awards and has also received many other music awards. Not only is Usher successful in the music business, he is also a community volunteer and businessman. In 2005, Usher was involved in many exciting projects. He developed a charity for young people, became one of the owners of a professional basketball team, and started his own record company!

Here is Usher at the 2004 Billboard Music Awards. Usher won 11 awards, including Artist of the Year.

An Early Music Career

Usher Raymond IV was born on October 14, 1978, to Usher Raymond III and Jonnetta Patton. He grew up singing in a local church **choir** in Chattanooga, Tennessee. When he was 12, he moved to Atlanta, Georgia, with his mom and brother, James. Many people recognized Usher's talent when he sang in an Atlanta church choir. After Usher performed in a local talent show in 1993, he got an **audition** with record producer Antonio "L.A." Reid. Reid knew that Usher had talent and signed him to a recording contract with his company, LaFace Records. Usher's first single was "Call Me Mack."

Usher and his mom are shown here in New York City at the opening of one of Usher's movies. Usher once said his mom is his best friend. She has been his manager for many years.

Usher's First Album

Usher's first album, called *Usher*, came out in August 1994. The album climbed to number 25 on the R&B charts. The single "Think of You" made it to the top 10 on the R&B/**Hip-Hop** charts. Although the album did not sell as well as expected, producers believed in Usher's talent. Usher continued to build his **reputation** as a singer by recording national **jingles** for a major soft drink company and for the 1996 Summer Olympics in Atlanta. Usher formed a vocal group called Black Men United and recorded a song called "U Will Know." It reached number 5 on the R&B/Hip-Hop charts in 1994.

Usher's career in music began with the release of his first album. He soon started receiving offers to make appearances and perform with other recording artists.

My Way

Shortly after he graduated from high school, Usher recorded his second album, *My Way*. He cowrote six of the songs on the album. The hit single "You Make Me Wanna" became popular even before the album was released in October 1997. It set a record by staying on the R&B charts for 71 weeks! Usher received his first Grammy Award **nomination** for this song in the category of Best Male R&B Vocal Performance. A second single, "Nice and Slow," also climbed the charts quickly and was praised for its music video. The success of this album helped Usher get more recognition as a talented singer and performer.

Usher is shown here with producer Jermaine Dupri. Dupri worked with Usher on two of his albums. Usher said that many of the songs on *My Way* were about his life as a teenager who was becoming an adult.

Usher Is Everywhere!

The popularity of *My Way* brought Usher offers to tour with Janet Jackson and other well-known singers. He appeared in music videos and also received many acting opportunities. Usher first appeared in the popular television show *Moesha* with singer-actress Brandy. In 1998, Usher got his first movie role in a film called *The Faculty*. He played a high school football player who discovers that his teachers are from another planet! In 1999, he appeared in a funny movie about teenagers called *She's All That*. In the same year, Usher got his first starring role in *Light It Up*. It's about a group of **urban** high school students who struggle to make changes in their school.

Usher is shown here dancing in a music video. He also danced in the TV movie *Geppetto* in 2000.

Live

Usher's performances and appearances on television made him popular with fans. They wanted to hear more music from him. In 1999, he released the *Live* album that included his top hits and live concert performances. **Remixes** of some old favorites, such as "My Way" and "You Make Me Wanna," were included on the album. The song "Just Like Me" featured vocals from Lil' Kim. Other guest artists who performed background vocals on the *Live* album included Jagged Edge, Shanice, Trey Lorenz, and Twista. *Live* reached number 30 on the R&B/Hip-Hop charts.

The *Live* album featured many of the songs that had made Usher so popular by 1999.

8701

On August 7, 2001, Usher released his fourth album, called *8701*. This album included several **ballads** and some hip-hop songs. Two hit singles from the album, "U Remind Me" and "U Got It Bad," reached number 1 on the music charts in the United States and held that spot for several weeks. The album was also successful in other countries. It reached number 1 in the United Kingdom and Canada. Usher won a Grammy Award for Best Male R&B Vocal Performance for "U Remind Me" in 2002. He also won a Grammy the next year for "U Got It Bad."

Usher has described himself as a rapper who sings. He said that he likes to tell stories in his songs.

17

More Movies

With another successful album, Usher could have taken a break. However, he decided to continue working as an actor. In 2001, he costarred in a movie called *Texas Rangers,* which was set in Texas in 1875. Usher played one of a group of men chosen to be Texas Rangers. Together, they fought outlaws to protect their homes and loved ones. In 2005, he starred in a movie called *In the Mix*. Usher played a nightclub DJ who became a bodyguard. Between recording albums and concert tours, Usher still finds time to work in movies.

Usher poses with costars Chazz Palminteri (far left), Iris Faust (left), and Emmanuelle Chriqui from the movie *In the Mix*.

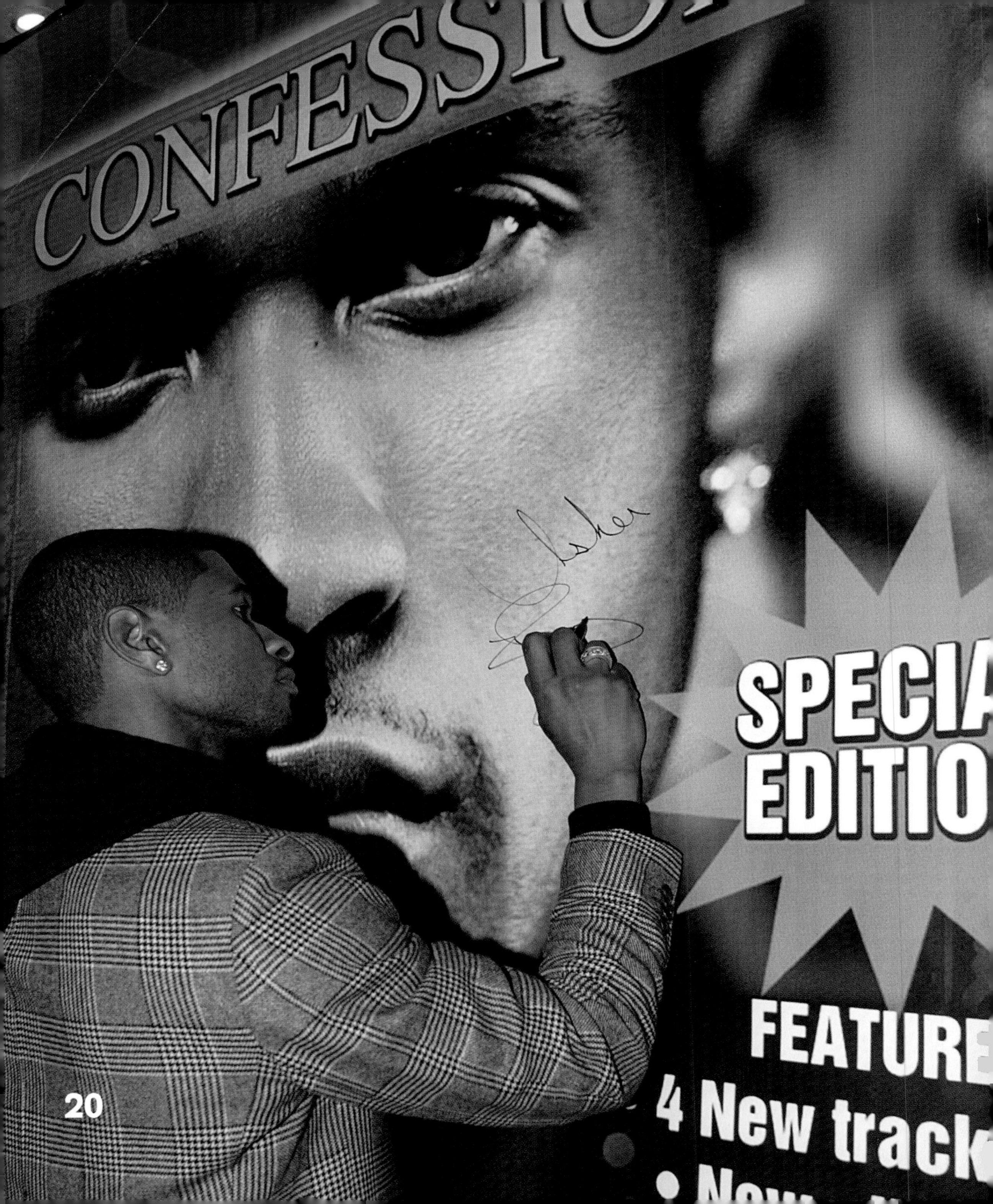
CONFESSIO
SPECIA
EDITIO
FEATURE
4 New track

Confessions

Usher released his fifth album, *Confessions*, in 2004. *Confessions* sold more than 1 million copies within the first week of its release. This album set a record for the highest sales by an R&B artist. The most successful single—called "Yeah!"—features Usher and rappers Ludacris and Lil' Jon. The songs "Burn" and "Confessions Part II" both topped the Billboard Hot 100 and R&B charts in the United States. A fourth single, "My Boo," features Usher and singer Alicia Keys. Usher won three Grammy Awards in 2005 for this album.

Usher signs a poster for his hit album *Confessions.*

Usher's New Look

In 2005, Usher started an organization for children called Usher's New Look. It was created to give kids ages 9 to 17 a chance to learn more about jobs in sports and entertainment. Usher's New Look runs a camp at Clark Atlanta University in Atlanta, Georgia. The camp offers 2 weeks of education and training to kids who want a career in singing, dancing, acting, screenwriting, or sports. Usher said he wants to give back to the community and help kids learn from his experiences.

Usher is shown here talking about Usher's New Look. Camp New Look offers workshops and training by top leaders in sports and entertainment.

23

Cleveland Cavaliers

Usher likes to stay busy and take on new business opportunities. He was excited when he had a chance to become one of the owners of a professional basketball team. In March 2005, Usher and a group of other businessmen purchased the Cleveland Cavaliers basketball team in Cleveland, Ohio. David Katzman, one of the other owners, said that Usher is the "ultimate entertainer" and plans to develop the entertainment part of the business. Usher said he wants to be actively involved with the team and the community of Cleveland.

Usher's love of basketball led him to become one of the owners of the Cleveland Cavaliers basketball team.

US Records

Usher worked for 3 years to develop his own record **label** called US Records. The sound track for the movie *In the Mix* was released on this label in November 2005. Usher worked as a songwriter and producer for this project but only sings on one of the songs. The sound track of original songs features rapper Rico Love and R&B **quintet** One Chance. Several other recording artists also performed on the sound track. Usher said that his main purpose for wanting his own label is to offer opportunities for artists who are building a career in the music business.

Many of the songs on the *In the Mix* sound track have been described as hip-hop dance music.

A Volunteer

Usher often volunteers his time to worthwhile community activities. He and other **celebrities** volunteered for the U.S. Department of Transportation's *Get Big on Safety* campaign. Usher has given safety messages about the importance of wearing seat belts and not drinking and driving. He has also performed in the National Basketball Association's *Stay in School* program and talked about the importance of education. Usher also took part in the NBA's *Read to Achieve* events that encouraged children to read. Usher has devoted a lot of time to providing positive opportunities for children.

Usher is shown here singing and dancing onstage during the 2003 NBA All-Star event "*Read to Achieve*," held in Atlanta, Georgia, in 2003.

What's Next for Usher?

Usher has used his talents in many ways throughout his life. In the future, he plans to continue singing, dancing, and acting. Usher always has new projects and goals for himself. He continues to appear in movies. He plays an R&B singer in *The Ballad of Walter Holmes*, released in 2006. Usher will also star in a movie about swing dancing called *Step in the Name of Love*. He is working on songs for a new album as well. Usher's energy, drive, and willingness to help others will continue to make him successful in whatever he does.

Glossary

audition (aw-DIH-shun) A short performance to test the talents of a singer, actor, or dancer.

ballad (BA-luhd) A slow, simple song that tells a story.

celebrity (suh-LEH-bruh-tee) Someone who is famous.

choir (KWYR) An organized group of singers.

critic (KRIH-tihk) A person who makes or gives a judgment about the value, worth, beauty, or quality of something.

hip-hop (HIHP–hahp) A type of music and dance associated with rap music.

jingle (JIHN-guhl) A short song that rhymes or repeats phrases in a catchy way.

label (LAY-buhl) A brand of music recordings issued by a company.

nomination (nah-muh-NAY-shun) The act of choosing someone as a candidate for a certain honor.

producer (pruh-DOO-suhr) A person who oversees something or provides money for it and gets it ready for public presentation.

quintet (kwihn-TEHT) A group of five.

remix (REE-mihks) A change or addition to an original recording.

reputation (reh-pyuh-TAY-shun) Good name.

urban (UHR-buhn) Of or relating to a city.

Index

Web Sites

Due to the changing nature of Internet links, PowerKids Press has develope an online list of Web sites related to the subject of this book. This site is updated regularly. Please use this link to access the list:
http://www.powerkidslinks.com/stars/usher/